AROUND THE WORLD

GREAT BRITAIN

First published in 1997 in the USA by
Thunder Bay Press
5880 Oberlin Drive, Suite 400
San Diego, CA 92121

ISBN 1 57145 085 8

Library of Congress Cataloging-in-Publication Data available upon request

Editions of this book will appear simultaneously
in France, Germany, Great Britain, Italy, Spain
and Holland under the auspices of
Euredition bv, Den Haag, Netherlands

Translated from the French by Burrett/Wiemeyer
Typesetting: Buro AD, Amersfoort
Printed by AUBIN IMPRIMEUR, Poitiers, France

AROUND THE WORLD

GREAT BRITAIN

Jean-Yves Montagu

THUNDER BAY
P·R·E·S·S

INTRODUCTION

1000 kilometres from north to south, 500 kilometres at its widest point, Great Britain – England, Wales and Scotland – covers a total area of 228,269 square kilometres and has a population of 56.1 million people.

History tells us that the Saxons and the German Angles invaded the south of the island in the 6th century. After years of bloody raids by the Picts from Ireland, the Scots Celts departed to settle in Scotland in the 5th century. The Welsh are also Celts, and their name 'Welsh' means 'stranger' in the language of the Saxons. Romans, Vikings and Normans have also occupied the country. Today their descendants are all 'British', although the three countries have quite distinct cultures and traditions.

ENGLAND

Verlaine found England much more amusing than France or Italy. In Bournemouth the celebrated French poet wrote "It was one of those times I love so much, neither mist nor sun! Only a sense of the sun's promise." For England is first a land of poetry, a land which has inspired

more than one artist. The landscapes painted by Constable can still be seen today in the southern area of East Anglia, which was also Gainsborough's birthplace.

The Italian, Canaletto, was besotted by the Thames and Turner himself said the light had a capriciousness that was typically English.

From Northumbria to Cornwall and in the South East, England has developed – 30 minutes away by ferry and 35 by the Channel tunnel – a programme of discoveries which marry history, the environment and the art of life.

It is true that life is sweet in the south of England and the number of great houses and castles are witness to the pleasure the aristocracy found in their summer quarters. Many of them have been inhabited by the same families for three or four centuries. Sevenoaks, for example, has always been the property of the Sackville Wests and is a veritable monument with 365 rooms, 12 staircases and 7 terraces... The park which surrounds it is populated by deer living in complete freedom. They are so numerous and so tame that a notice asks visitors not to feed them.

Magic is always in the air in Merlin's Cave, at the rocks of Stonehenge or at Bath with its Roman thermal baths built to survive the centuries. The north of England is closely linked to the Industrial Revolution, but it would be a mistake to underestimate this region with its old docklands and restored factories. Chester, a ravishing Tudor city in black and white, a neighbour of Liverpool, or Yorkshire, the heart of the Peak District, the wild uplands of the Pennines where Haworth is, where one discovers the world of the Brontë sisters and the passion of Wuthering Heights.

The heart of England is Shakespeare, Robin Hood, and the 'must' universities which have brought England such fame; or London, glittering in a light which has nothing to do with its charm as the capital city. "A summer Sunday, when the sun breaks through, London is a pleasure for the connaisseur", Victor Hugo wrote.

proverb: 'An Englishman's home is his castle', has a Welsh counterpart: 'The Welshman's castle is his playground'.

The Celtic civilization made a great impression on the Romans, who conscripted the Welsh into their legions, but massacred the Druids. This genocide took place on the Isle of Anglesey, off the north coast of Wales. The Druids possessed much social and religious power – and economic power, too. In effect, they had finally centralized the commerce in gold, which the Romans took over.

Druids and bards followed an apprenticeship which might have lasted twenty years, the last of which were spent memorizing the law texts and many epic poems. In order to preserve their power and prevent it falling into the wrong hands, these men of culture, noted for their wisdom, were not in the habit of writing things down. Fortunately, a number of poems, written in medieval Welsh and dating from the VIth century, have been preserved.

The arrival of Christianity in Great Britain coincided with the disappearance of the Druid cast and with the amena (the age of saints) which resulted in the foundation of the Celtic Church. While Europe was falling prey to the barbarians, Wales (like Ireland) was developing into a brilliant civilization.

The Celts considered water to be sacred. This is witnessed by the numerous springs and fountains dedicated to the saints. The people accorded so much importance to their natural environment that every letter of their alphabet corresponded to a tree. Moreover, wild animals played a large role in Celtic beliefs. They often integrated themselves so much into the land-

WALES

Though geographically it shares a common border with England, Wales has its own specific character. The Welsh language is spoken by more than 20% of the population and understood by many more. Then there is the countryside, the most verdent in the world. In Welsh, the word 'green' can be translated in many ways. It should be noted that just as most of the rivers have retained their Celtic name, so, too, the Avon which evokes Shakespeare, derives its name from the Welsh 'arfon', which means 'river'.

Wales has the reputation of having more castles per square kilometre than any other country in Europe. Whether this reputation is merited or not, the castles *are* numerous there. The English

scape that certain names have survived to the present day. 'Pant y Glas', for example, means 'the Valley of the Mare'. The Welsh countryside has a rare beauty; numerous parks have been created for the protection of the landscape. In addition to the three National Parks (the Brecon Beacons, Snowdonia and the coast of Pembrokeshire), there are a large number of classified areas – the Isle of Anglesey, the Gower peninsula, the valley of the River Wye, the Llyn peninsula and the mountains of Clwyd. Moreover, the sea is always very close to Wales and the five regions all have access to the sea. Two thirds of the Welsh coast is classified as heritage coastline and benefits from special protection. Agriculture is the pivot of economic activity and there are three times as many sheep as there are people. And lastly, there are the numerous associations, public and private, employed in the protection of the flora and fauna, and the inhabitants.

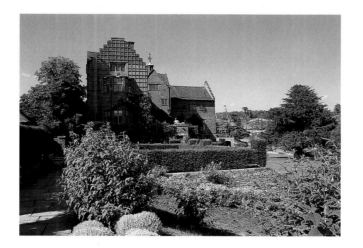

SCOTLAND

"If I could live in a country I love, I would go to live in Scotland. It is a country I love because of its mysteries. There are rainstorms and there are mists, it is thinly populated and there are great stretches of virgin landscape," Jean Giono wrote. Scotland covers an area of 78,650 square kilometres and consists of two groups of mountains, the Highlands and the Southern Uplands, separated by a collapsed basin, the Lowlands. The land of the Scots (Celts originating from Ireland) is a raw and savage country where nature has preserved its rights and all its charm. Enclosed on three sides by the sea and girded with a chain of islands and rocky islets, the land of Walter Scott, Mary Stuart and whisky is a vast territory of powerful inspiration where the sea, the rocks, the clouds merge into a grand backdrop which forms the soul of a profoundy original country.

The present-day Scots are the issue of a fusion of many peoples – the Caledonians or Picts, the Scots, the Bretons, the Angles and the Vikings. For long independent, the Kingdom of Scotland joined with the Kingdom of England in 1603, when King James VI of Scotland also became King James I of England.

In 1707, the union of the two parliaments consecrated unity – without bringing about total assimilation. On this point, George Bernard Shaw stated that the Scots were incompatible with British civilization.

It should be recalled that France has maintained privileged links with the Scots over the centuries. In the 15th century, notably, the 'Auld Alliance' allowed the passage of Scottish troops who contributed to 'booting' the English out of the Kingdom of Lys. The Constable (Field Marshal) of the armies of Charles VII was also Scots, and the victory of Baugé (Maine-et-Loire) in 1421 raised great hopes when Joan of Arc entered the fray. A century later, dual nationality came about between the two countries and Mary Stuart entered into legend. Innumerable castles still witness those mythical times when Scotland cut a figure of grandeur and was an example to Europe. What remains are the costumes, the traditions and a force of character which ignores half measures and cultivates a nobility of soul, whose principle characteristics are a spirit of independence, an appetite for life and a sense of the epic.

OXFORD

Specialized in the art of academic living ever since the 12th century. In fact, the famous Oxford university was founded in 1167, when during the particularly turbulent Middle Ages, the Sorbonne closed its doors to foreigners thereby forcing students to retreat across the Channel. In 1214 a papal decree was issued in order to sooth the minds of the initially hostile, rebellious young people who disturbed the quiet life of sleepy market towns along the rivers Thames and Cherwell. It is interesting to know that since its foundation, Oxford University has always relied on royal support, which became even stronger in the 14th century with a new decree firmly establishing its judicial powers.

The charm of Oxford is the result of a wise mix of elegance and tradition. From Christ Church, founded in 1525 by Cardinal Wolsey, to the Venetian bridge constructed in 1903 over Queen's Lane, which joins the old and new buildings of Herford College, Oxford allows you to discover the most prestigious colleges of the Kingdom: Merton College, Magdalen College, Bailliol College, St. Johns College, Lincoln College, etc. This visit starts at Carfax. About 13.000 students come to Oxford each year: 8.000 men and 5.000 women, the latter being admitted since the 19th century. It is a place where cricket and rowing remain the sporting pillars of every gentleman.

Above: Christchurch Cricket Club.
Opposite page: Lincoln College, one
of the great colleges of Oxford.
Following page: Windsor Castle
dominates the right bank of the
Thames.

WINDSOR

Principal residence of British kings since William the Conqueror, Windsor Castle dominates the right bank of the Thames. In the olden days it had been built as a wooden fortress to defend the Thames against invasions, and during the 12th and 13th centuries it became surrounded by ramparts. In the 19th century, George IV and Queen Victoria spent one million pounds on the renovation of the apartments, enlarged by Charles II earlier. The renovation of St. George Chapel also dates from the 19th century. Dedicated to the holy patron of the Order of Garter, this chapel is the last remains of the Gothic style. The Order of the Garter finds its origin in 1318 when the Countess of Salisbury, dancing with the king during a ball, lost one of her garters. Being the gallant man he was, the king picked it up and exclaimed: "Honni soit qui mal y pense," or "Evil to him who thinks evil." The Order of the Garter was established right there and then.

The state rooms in the north wing of the castle are reserved for visiting heads of state.

In the south, Windsor Park stretches for more than 10 kilometres and 800 hectares. Even further south lie the Valleys Gardens, which are especially worth a visit during the months of April, May and June, when the azaleas and rhododendrons are in bloom. Worth mentioning are the facts that the changing of the guards is more spectacular at Windsor than at Buckingham Palace and that one of the most famous schools in Britain, Eton, is located right on the other side of the Thames.

STONEHENGE

As one of the most spectacular pre-historic monuments in Europe, this great landmark in Britain is a genuine Megalithic structure. The roughly tailored cross beams rest on upright stones. The structure dates from the second millennium before Christ, at the beginning of the Bronze Age and is supposed to have succeeded an even older structure.

The pattern consists of an outer ring and inner horse-shoe of stone. In the middle lies a massive stone, formally considered as a sacrificial altar, pointing towards the horizon where the sun shines during the Midsummer day. The smaller stones, placed in south-eastern and north-eastern directions indicate the point of sunrise on Midwinter days.

The blue stones in the big circle originate from the Preseli hills in the south-east of Wales more than 200 kilometres away. Although these hills are to a large extent accessible by ship, this does in no way diminish the perseverance of the people who constructed Stonehenge at the time. In fact, the importance and solemnity of the structure present technical problems which are hard to understand.

The only known temple from the occidental Neolithic period, apart from similar structures on Malta, Stonehenge still does not reveal its secrets, although quite a number of specialists claim that the Neolites worshipped the sun. But should one look for evidence of a true sun cult? The question remains unanswered, even if, to this day, the rites of the druids are still being performed a few days after Midsummer day.

*Previous pages: The megalithic
structure of Stonehenge dates from
the Bronze Age.*

DORCHESTER

It is in his 19th century novel 'The Mayor of Casterbridge', that novelist Thomas Hardy made his native Dorset famous, in describing its economic and social changes.

Dorchester, where the ramparts constructed by the Romans have been replaced by a round boulevard lined by trees, until this day shows quite a number of remains of its onetime glory. This can best be seen on buildings on High East and High West Streets dating from the 18th and 19th centuries. Thomas Hardy's cottage can be visited in the hamlet of Higher Brockhampton at 5 kilometres from Dorchester. In any case the most important curiosity of Dorchester is the Dorset Country Museum, in which Roman antiquities and pre-historic objects are exhibited. A military museum dedicated to the famous Dorset regiment founded in 1702 is also worth a visit.

WEYMOUTH

At Weymouth one is able to embark for the Channel Islands and Cherbourg. Weymouth owes its reputation to George II who while very ill in 1789, spent quite a long time in this town. It is said that when the king bathed in full dress the music of 'God Save George, Our King' was played. This seaside resort combines a large beach and water works hidden in a shielded bay.

Top: The ancient port of Weymouth.
Above and opposite page:
Dorchester.

Above: The resort of Shanklin.

*Opposite page: The picturesque
cottages of Old Shanklin.*

*Previous pages: The Needles on the
west coast of the Isle of Wight.*

ISLE OF WIGHT

A diamond-shaped piece of land of 377 km^2 – open in the south to the Channel and closed off at the north side by the Solent – where each year the famous international regattas take place.

Thanks to its mild climate, it is an ideal holiday retreat. During the 19th century Queen Victoria often came to the island for prolonged visits. The south coast alternately offers hidden beaches and high cliffs, which in the west stretch out into the sea in the shape of a couple of large rocks with spectacular tops, called The Needles. On the much more hospitable coast in the north, Cowes is famous for its prestigious Cowes Week, which for sailing is what Ascot is for horse racing.

The capital Newport, situated at the end of the Medina estuary, dates from Norman ages. At 25 kilometres south west, Carisbrook castle has been built on the site of a Roman fortress. Charles I was imprisoned here for one year before he was brought to London for his trial, death sentence and subsequent execution.

In the south west, the sea-side resort Shanklin has an old town, Old Shanklin, where one can still see the picturesque thatched houses. At 8 kilometres in the direction of Newport lies Godshill, a lovely village with thatched houses still honoring the tradition of signboards. Its Gothic church dates from the 14th century.

Above: Scotney Castle and its celebrated flower gardens.
Right: Chartwell, once the home of Sir Winston Churchill.
Opposite page: top, Chiddingford Church; bottom, characteristic green meadows of Kent.

KENT COUNTRYSIDE

Sleepy villages, castles, hidden gardens and green pastures are the characteristics of Kent.

Situated in the south-east of Britain, this region also carries the marks of the invaders who attempted to take possession of the island. Beautiful churches embody the spirit of its people who attached great value to their identity and the protection of it. Westerham village bears witness to the presence in the region of two important figures in the history of Britain: General Wolfe and Sir Winston Churchill. Quebec House – where General Wolfe lived as a child – and Squerryes Court, a manor dating from the 17th century, both contain objects associated with Wolfe's family and the battle of Quebec. Chartwell, on the other hand, the property of Sir Winston Churchill, has remained unchanged since the death of this illustrious statesman.

Scotney castle, dating from the 14th century, is built on an island in the middle of magnificent grounds. It was partly destroyed in 1905.

The history of Owl House gardens also goes back a long way and is full of adventures. More than six hectares of ornamental fruit trees, scrubs and fields of flowers surround the four-hundred-years-old cave used by wool smugglers, known as 'Owlers'.

BRIGHTON

Once upon a time there was a poor fishing village which as if by magic turned into a prestigious sea-side resort. The wand through which this transformation came about has been carefully preserved in the archives. It is a medical publication entitled: 'Dissertation on the use of sea water in the treatment of lymphatic diseases'. It was written in 1750 and its author, doctor Russell, is the first known doctor to have recommended bathing in the sea.

In 1785 George IV gave the new resort his royal blessing and the spa guests started arriving. At the beginning of the 19th century, a real construction boom took hold of the town. Completely new districts emerged in Regency style. Promenade piers towered over the waves and the Royal Pavilion became the

epitome of the Mongol spirit. John Nash, its architect, had in fact been inspired by the Mongol palaces in India for the outside architecture and interior decorations. The Chinese apartments inside the Pavilion are open to the public.

The main pier, Palace Pier, was built in 1898. It holds a theatre, a dancing and various popular entertainment facilities.

For those who look for peace and quiet and nature, the Seven Sisters Country Park, at 16 kilometres, is the right place: a natural park situated above seven white cliffs (The Seven Sisters), which dominate the Channel.

Above: the Palace Pier at Brighton. Opposite page: The Royal Pavilion, inspired by the Mogul palaces of India.

Following pages: The Seven Sisters Country Park above seven white cliffs (the seven sisters) which dominate the Channel.

PORTSMOUTH

Capital of the Royal Navy, this Hampshire port beholds the glorious souvenirs of Admiral Nelson, who won the battle of Trafalgar in 1805. From dockyards at Chatham near London, The Victory was launched on May 7, 1765. The ship's career was an impressive one. After having participated in the landing at Toulon in 1793, followed by Corsica in 1794, it became the flag ship under Nelson. In this capacity The Victory appeared on September 15, 1805 near the Spanish coast, where on October 21, 1805, it fought its most important battle, not far from Cape Trafalgar. Armed with 104 guns, she had 850 officers and crew aboard. Once back in Portsmouth the famous ship would never again leave the docks. After having undergone a restoration in 1922, it is now open to the public – more or less in the state it was during the battle of Trafalgar.

Portsmouth, which remains the principal naval base of the Royal Navy, cultivates its maritime memory in a famous marine museum. The figurehead of the Hibernia is proof of the symbolic naval architecture in sailing ships.

The church of St. Thomas of Canterbury, built in the 12th century en enlarged in the 17th century, can be found on High Street. Inside one can admire a model of the Mary Rose, the ship of Henry VIII.

Top and opposite page: The Victory of the Battle of Trafalgar, today open to the public.
Above left: Portsmouth Cathedral.
Above right: The figure-head of the Hibernia.

SURREY

George Perec once wrote: "It is easy to just travel on the main highways: but with a minimum of experience and a sense of adventure, it is just as easy to look for a little happiness (...) which, depending on the travel time needed and the weather, could be found through a somewhat erratic itinerary, on more or less winding roads, with beacons of evocative places, even if one does not know exactly what they remind one of."

Surrey, in the middle of Britain, is ideal for this kind of travelling. Its murmuring river, undoubtedly painted by Constable, a site for unexpected encounters. From a barge one is able to discover a landscape with villages and typical curiosities: from a windmill to a historic village with its pub on the waterfront, deep into the countryside, Britain reveals its secret charms. "The trees and mills are as feathers on the tender pastures," Verlaine wrote about this area.

Above: The river Wey in Surrey, land of river rambles.
Opposite page: Flat-bottomed boats on the Wey.

CAMBRIDGE

Before Cambridge became known as a university town, it was a place where several religious orders had established themselves. It was because of violent disagreements with the population of Oxford that a number of students and professors came to Cambridge in the 13th century, at a time when this town already enjoyed an intellectual reputation. Owing to the generosity of the nobility, the newly constructed buildings of the university radiated a cultural atmosphere throughout Europe.

The teachings of Erasmus between 1511 and 1513 at Queen's College were decisive for the propagation of the ideas of the Reformation. Today Cambridge University, formed by an amalgamation of 29 colleges, is largely independent.

Trinity College was founded by Henry VIII in 1546 and houses a library built in Italian Renaissance style. The interior of the chapel is

Above: The lawns and the facade of King's College.
Right: The Gothic Chapel of Trinty College.
Opposite page: top left, the clock of Trinity College; top right, punt on the river Cam; bottom, Saint John's College.

Gothic, and its 18th century wood-work absolutely remarkable.

King's College was founded in 1441 by Henry VI. The charm of its gardens and the beauty of its chapels are well known.

St.John's College, founded in 1511 by Lady Margaret Beaufort, has a main gate decorated with animal heraldic sculptures. The architectural structure is impressive thanks to its homogeneity and power. Behind it, the Bridge of Sighs over the river Cam evokes curious connotations with Venice, but even if the gondolas are much more spartan, its amorous purpose remains the same.

STRATFORD

Every year 'Shakespeare's village' attracts thousands of visitors who come in pilgrimage to the place were the great playwright lived, worked and died. The Shakespeare birthday celebration takes place in April and the Stratford Festival in July.

William Shakespeare was born on April 23, 1564 and died on April 23, 1616 in Stratford, where he is buried in the parish church. In the chancel set of the Holy Trinity Church is a bust of Shakespeare.

BATH

Bath owes its reputation to the hot springs, discovered by the Romans, who built temples and baths on the site. In the Roman Bath Museum, excavated at the end of the 19th century, a bronze head of Minerva, mosaics and a head of Medusa can be admired. Bath preserves the architectural style inspired by Andrea Palladio, Italian architect of the Renaissance. The originators of this elegant urban landscape, built in the 18th century, are two architects: John Wood father and son.

Royal Crescent is a perfect voluptuous illustration of this Palladian inspiration, en vogue with the then British jet-set. Its immense neo-classic facade looks out over a park.

Opposite page: Holy Trinity Church at Stratford which contains a monument erected to the glory of Shakespeare.
Top: The theatre of Bath.
Above: The Palladian architecture of the Royal Crescent at Bath.

*Above: The overhanging cliffs of the
Lizard Point on the coast of
Cornwall.*
*Opposite page: The fishing village of
Polperro, famous for its celebrated
cream teas.*

CORNWALL/DEVON

This rocky land near Cape Lizard is impressive through both its wildness and its enchanting beauty. Land's End, the most western point of Britain, is a country of legends and strange customs. The Atlantic coast and the oceanic adventure begin right here. In line with the nature surrounding them, the inhabitants are strong, serene and of poetic temperament. Cornwall is the country of King Arthur of Camelot (his mythical castle) and the Holy Grail, after all. Tintagel Castle, dating from the 12th century, is situated on top of an isolated rock in the sea. Legend has it that King Arthur was born there. In the southeast St.Ives arises from a single rock, its beautiful lighting until this day attracting painters from all over the world. Its paved streets are packed with small shops and art galleries.

Polperro is a lovely fishing village. The cream tea which is served in the little whitewashed tearooms is a delicacy: scones with thick clotted cream and strawberry jam... Plymouth is the place where the Pilgrim fathers embarked on board the Mayflower; on the English Riviera, the palm trees and tropical flowers of Torquay, former hide out of smugglers, give an exotic smell to the birth place of Agatha Christie. The famous author was inspired by the island of Burgh when she wrote 'Evil under the Sun', one of her many famous books.

CORNWALL/DEVON

Daphne du Maurier once wrote: "There is a freedom here, a freedom which is part of the air and the sea." This peninsula has a wild Atlantic coast in the north and a sheltered one in the south. More than 800 kilometres of coast roads allow you to go from the high granite rocks to the depths of the estuaries where the fishing harbors and... painters are.

The coasts of this region provide the British people with several much-appreciated holiday resorts. Tourists are lured by the numerous attractions: golden beaches, surfing, sailing, fishing and the mild climate. The West Country, home to a number of stock-farms, also possesses two national parks: Dartmoor National Park and Exmoor National Park. Only furze and fern grow on the Dartmoor heights.

The moor is inhabited by ponies and sheep and crossed in every direction by glistering brooks. Alongside the roads one can still see remains of former civilizations: the bronze, the Roman and the early Christian one.

The churches have maintained their rustic authentic character and the secret magic of their original religions.

Opposite page and above: Two views of the verdant pastures of the high plateau of Dartmoor where sheep, horses and ponies graze.

YORKSHIRE

"In the north-west of Britain, York-shire offers a coastline with impressive cliffs and a landscape with in its onw way equally impressive faults," Robert Fish wrote on Yorkshire. Another remarkable aspect of the region is that it has held on to certain customs. For instance, each evening in the Ripon area, the shattered sheep find their way back thanks to the sound of a horn which can be heard all over the Yorkshire Dales (valleys).

A few kilometres from Ripon, one can admire an original variety of landscapes assembled in the Studley Royal garden. Before reaching the ruins of an abbey you will encounter a tiny Greek temple, hidden in the foliage. It was built in the middle of the 18th century. The river Skell has been transformed into waterfalls or basins in the middle of which replicas of antique ornaments add a Mediterranean touch to this English garden. The limestone mountains of York-shire have formed gorges through which rivers stream and waterfalls come down, such as the Rysgarth Falls.

Above: A green valley in the heart of Yorkshire.

Opposite page: top, construction in the form of a Greek temple in the gardens of Studley Royal; bottom, the cascades of Rysgarth Falls.

YORKSHIRE

Seat of the Primate of Britain, York is heir to a long economic and political history. During Saxon times, this famous town was the cultural capital before it became the commercial centre of the northern part of Britain. Its cathedral dedicated to St. Peter is one of Britain's architectural jewels. The building testifies to the evolution of English Gothicism. Its construction started in the 13th century, taking until the 15th century to be completed. The transepts, nave, chapter, choir and towers are Gothic.

While York is undeniably an example of a medieval town which has been remarkably well preserved, it also offers the National Railway Museum which contains the largest railway collection in Britain.

In the middle of a park lies Fountains Abbey, a cisterian house, formerly one of the richest in Britain. It reincarnates the past splendors of the European monastic order of Saint

Above: York Minster.
Right: The lake of Studley Royal.
Opposite page: top, the cellarium of Fountains Abbey; bottom, Castle Howard, celebrated for its collection of old masters.

Bernard. The chapter which leans on the southside of the church is still beautifully preserved. It is 90 meters long and 12 meters wide and is divided into two naves.

Castle Howard, home of the Howard family, is a English Baroque castle dating from the 18th century. It holds a collection of old masters, English and Dutch furniture from the 18th and 19th centuries and a costume collection from the 18th century until today.

LAKE DISTRICT

The Lake District is the most poetic region of Britain, and brought forth William Wordsworth, the most famous of the 'lake poets', who at the end of the 18th century and during the 19th century sung of the simple and romantic joys of going back to nature.

The Lake District is a small region (50 kilometres from north to south and 30 kilometres from east to west), with a rich soul and many traditions.

on the river Derwent from its garden is particularly beautiful. Going south one reaches Buttermere Lake. The tourist industry of the Lake District is based on a well-balanced socio-economic policy, which permits farmers to stay loyal to their traditions and to take care of a privileged region in exemplary harmony.

Above and opposite page: Lake Buttermere on the southerly route in the Lake District.
Right and below: The river Derwent so well-loved by the poet William Wordsworth.

It is interesting to know that Britain's three highest mountains all are located in this district. The places worth visiting in the Lake District are not only interesting from a geological or ecological point of view, but the many museums offering a wide range of exhibitions, excitement and entertainment will also satisfy those looking for cultural enjoyment.

But above all this region is unique for the vastness of water, known to have inspired many artists. The birthplace of William Wordsworth can still be visited in Cockermouth. The view

TRAFALGAR SQUARE

Trafalgar Square honors the victory of Nelson in 1805, which took place in an era when Britain was at the peak of its glory and ruled the waves. On top of a 51 metres high granite Corynthian column stands the statue of this great British admiral. Meeting point and former gathering place for huge crowds, Trafalgar Square is a mythical spot where in the olden days many political rallies took place.

Since the 18th century, no. 10 Downing Street is the official residence of Britain's Prime Minister. In 1731 the house was presented by George II to his prime minister Robert Walpole. The adjoining houses are occupied by other members of government.

Top: Trafalgar Square in London and its celebrated granite column.
Above: 10 Downing Street, official residence of the Prime Minister.
Opposite page: top, the Covent Garden quarter; bottom, Piccadilly Circus.

PICCADILLY CIRCUS

Piccadilly Circus, famous for its bronze statue of Eros, where large crowds of tourists used to gather, has now become a very busy square with lots of traffic. However, at nightfall it regains some of its old charm, when all the neon signs on the surrounding buildings are switched on.

COVENT GARDEN

Covent Garden used to be the vegetable garden of Westminster Abbey, where during many centuries, the covered market of London was located. In the eighties it was converted into a district of restaurants, artists, cafes and luxury shops.

LONDON PUBS

Most of the pubs date from the puritan Victorian days, when selling drinks gave these Public Houses a certain air of decency. Today, some of the pubs offer musical entertainment or striptease. Many are just local hangouts, some have an aristocratic atmosphere, others... a bad reputation.

The pubs serve British beer, ale or bitter, and still adhere to the rule that a good beer is draught beer served at cellar temperature, despite the fact that today foreign beer is served ice-cold as well.

Formerly, the pubs used to brew their own beer. One of the last ones still holding on to this tradition has a name which in itself is a poem: 'The ferret and firkin in the balloon up the crock.' It is impossible to translate this, as the word 'firkin' does not exist anymore and 'up the creek' does not only mean 'over the river', but also a 'difficult dangerous situation.'

The pub is an institution, the opening hours of which are subject to regulations. It is selected by the Londoner for its guests and the atmosphere. The latter is influenced by the interior, and the frame of mind of its guests. Since about twenty years, the wine bars, half pub-half restaurant, are trying to compete, but they will never equal the typically British comfort and warmth of the Public Houses.

Above and opposite page: Various pubs in London where it is the custom to serve hand-drawn beer at cellar temperature.

47

WESTMINSTER ABBEY

The most symbolic religious edifice of Britain. In fact all the British sovereigns were crowned and buried there. Also quite a number of illustrious persons, who have contributed to the glory of the Kingdom, are laid to rest inside Westminster Abbey. From an architectural point of view, Westminster is a sample of Gothicism. It was built in the 13th century in a primitive Gothic style during the better part of Henry III's reign. In the 15th century it obtained its flamboyant ornaments and its many curves.

In the 16th century, Henry VII rebuilt the chapel, whose choir is extended according to the style of Perpendicular architecture. This represents the last phase of British Gothicism, characterized by the priority given to vertical rather than horizontal lines.

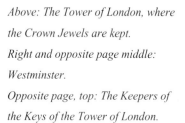

Above: The Tower of London, where the Crown Jewels are kept.
Right and opposite page middle: Westminster.
Opposite page, top: The Keepers of the Keys of the Tower of London.

THE TOWER OF LONDON

The Crown jewels are on display in the Tower of London. Originally built by William the Conqueror as a fortress, it became a royal residence and finally a state prison. Today, turned into a museum, it is a tourist attraction visited by masses of people who are eager to see the Crown jewels, among which the Star of Africa is considered the purest diamond in the world and the largest (530 carats). It was a gift to Edward II from the Union of South Africa. Since 700 years the Key Ceremony takes place every evening at 21.53 hours.

Above: Buckingham Palace, official
London residence of the Royal
Family.
Opposite page: top, the Horse
Guards; bottom, detail of the main
entrance of Buckingham Palace.

BUCKINGHAM PALACE

Buckingham Palace, official residence of the Royal Family in London, was originally built in the 18th century. It has lived through considerable transformations throughout the years. John Sheffield, Duke of Buckingham, was the first owner of the palace in 1703. It was purchased from him in 1762 by George III, when it became royal property. The imposing facade is made of Portland stone.

The Royal Standard flies above the building when the sovereign is in residence. The Queen's Gallery and the Royal Mews are open to the public.

The Changing of the Guards is the main attraction of Buckingham Palace. Every day at 11.30 hours, according to traditional custom, the Old Guard and the New Guard change keys accompanied by the sound of military music. The ceremony lasts about 30 minutes.

During official occasions, the Royal Family appears on the balcony to wave to the crowds of people, who push each other out of the way to get as close as possible behind the richly ornamented front gates.

The Horse Guards belong to an elite regiment, which has its quarters next to Whitehall. Every year on the Queen's birthday, these Horse Guards are responsible for a famous parade: Trooping the Colour.

Top: The Tate Gallery.

Above: The National Gallery.

Right: The Britsh Museum.

Opposite page: The National History Museum.

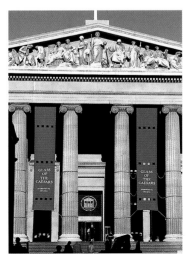

Following pages: The Houses of Parliament.

THE BRITISH MUSEUM

The British Museum exhibits six to seven million artifacts from every conceivable civilization and human interest source of the world. It is a marvel of classification and order which started with the legacy of Sir Hans Sloane, an 18th century naturalist/physician. When he died, he left the museum 80.000 rare objects, which he had collected during his entire life.

Amongst the exhibits are sculptures

The abundance and variety of paintings on display have forced the museum to extend. It is to be noted that the J.M. William Turner collection is exhibited in total. Among the 9000 portraits of unequalled artistic value in the National Portrait Gallery, the Royal Family occupies an important place.

from Pakistan, the Rosetta stone, which is used to decipher hieroglyphes, the archeopteryx, a fossil bird, etc.

TATE GALLERY, NATIONAL GALLERY

Built on the former site of the Millbanks penetentiary, the Tate Gallery, since its foundation in 1897, houses collections which have been donated to the Kingdom by Sir Henry Tate.

HOUSES OF PARLIAMENT

The Gothic style of the present Houses of Parliament is the work of Charles Barry and Augustus Pugin, and their pupils. The Parliament Chambers are occupied by the House of Commons and the House of Lords.

GARDENS AND PARKS IN LONDON

Kew Gardens, located on the south bank of the Thames behind Kew Bridge, is especially admired by botanists. Serpentine Park which seals off Serpentine Lake was laid out in 1730 for the Royal Family. Mary Shelley, wife of the famous poet, drowned in the lake and the victory of Nelson was commemorated there in 1814 with a spectacular reconstruction.

Hyde Park is famous for its large gatherings. 1851 is a symbolic date: it was in that year that the Great Exhibition was held which counted more than 6 million visitors. For this occassion the town had Crystal Palace built, the roof of which towers over the trees.

During the Sixties, carnivals and giant concerts succeeded each other. In the Middle Ages, the gallows could be found at the north-east side of the park. Before the executions the convicts had the right to speak up for the last time. Every Sunday on Speaker's corner, orators are more or less continuing this privilege by freely expressing their views on subjects of their choosing.

The gardens of London.
Opposite page: Kew Gardens.
This page: top, Hyde Park where it is the custom for orators to speak in public on Sundays; bottom, the Serpentine in Hyde Park.

THE WYE VALLEY

Touring the Wye used to be the obligatory journey of every romantic, the more so after William Wordsworth wrote his famous poem which was directly inspired by the region. The following lines were composed a few miles above Tintern Abbey:
And I felt
A presence which fills me with happiness
Sublime thoughts: a transcendental sensation
Of something so profoundly varied
Which is held in the light of the sunsets
In the vastness of the ocean and the air we breath, in the blue sky and in the spirit of man.

On one of the river banks of the Wye stands the Cisterian Abbey of Tintern. Founded in the 12th century by Walter Fitz Richard de Clare, Lord of Chepstow, it was the second of the 75 abbeys established by the order in Britain and Wales. The monks cultivated immensely vast grounds and owned a fleet which was based mainly in Bristol and Monmouth.

Monmouth, for a long time claimed by Britain, still shows signs of this centuries' old rivalry in a series of castles, which was built to defend the access to the valley. It is worth mentioning that Charles Rolls, co-founder of the famous Rolls Royce automobile company was born in this region.

Above: The countryside of Monmouth.
Opposite page: The river Wye (top), which shelters Tintern Abbey (bottom), founded by the Cistercians in the 12th century, on one of its banks.

BRECON BEACONS PARK

In days long gone its mysterious beauty made it the chosen grounds of the druids. Today, the national park of Brecon Beacons occupies 344 km^2 of mountains and grounds visited by many wanderers and, in some places, by the famous British SAS commando troops.

The red sandstone dominates and the highest point, Pen Y Fan (885 metres), offers a wonderful panorama of the conifer vegetation, from where many torrents flow towards the lakes which are reserved for water sports and fishing. These mountains are the breeding grounds of Welsh ponies, famous for their sturdiness and fine heads, inherited, so it has been said, from the battle horses of Roman troops. Four million sheep live freely in the park, but protective barbed wires have been put around the fields adjacent to the roads which connect the highlands with each other.

The two principal attractions of the park are the Dan-Yr-Ogof caves and the Dinosaur Park which contains life-size statues of dinosaurs.

Red sandstone dominates the mountains of the Brecon Beacons National Park (opposite), one of the regions where the Druids were chosen. One can visit the huge caves of Dan-Yr-Ogof and the Dinosaur Park.

CARDIFF

Capital of Wales, Cardiff is a harbour which used to have the worldwide export of coal and iron as its main activity. It is also the capital of rugby, where the famous Arms Park stadium, situated in the center of town, holds the rugby museum. Cardiff Castle, originally Norman, has a Roman foundation. In fact, it was built on the ruins of a Roman fortress which is still visible and was meant to control the local population which was extremely hostile to invadors. The dungeon was the work of the Normans, in particular William, who chose the site at the beginning of the 11th century. During the civil war of the 17th century, the structure was completely demolished. It was only until the 19th century and the third Marquis of Bute that important restoration works took place, to be completed in 1872.

In the Bell Tower houses the apartments of the castle where the Scottish

Above: Cardiff Castle, built on Roman foundations.
Right: The cathedral.
Opposite page: top left, the nave and choir of the cathedral; top right, one of the towers of the castle; below, the Arms Park rugby stadium.

crown is kept. It symbolises the origins of the Bute family who emigrated to Cardiff in the 17th century.

At 3 kilometres north-west from Cardiff, Llandaff cathedral embodies a religious tradition going back to the 6th century. A Celtic cross dating from the 10th century, serving as the basis of the present cathedral, reminds of the pre-Norman period. A parabolic arch, decorated with a modern sculpture by Jacob Epstein – Christ in all his glory – serves as the casing for the organ and dominates the central nave.

SWANSEA

During the 19th century, Swansea, second largest town of Wales, was the metallurgy capital of the world. Today, it features as the debarkation port for the ferries to Cork. It is a nice seaside town boasting considerable economic activity due to the refineries which are located next to the ironworks.

Its pleasure port holds 600 mooring sites. Moreover, the maritime district houses an Industry and Marine

moors and stories of lemmings plunging from the cliffs into the ocean. The sheep love to be at the Farm Museum at Llandevi and can also still be found on the moors.

Museum containing a floating oak trawler of 500 tons, a steam ship, a beacon ship and a restored war ship transformed into a restaurant and pub.

The Rhossili cliffs fringe a seaside strip of land which starts at Mumbles Point. Bays and creeks accomodates the lovers of surf and fine sand.

The Gower peninsula still echoes many Celtic mysteries, with Neolithic grave yards next to Druidic

This page middle and opposite page: The beaches and cliffs of the Gower Peninsula which shelter the Farm Museum (this page top).
Right: Swansea harbour.

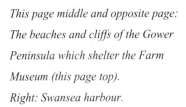

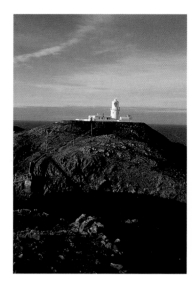

PEMBROKESHIRE COAST

This is one of the most beautiful coast lines of Britain, turned into a 260-kilometres-long national park. Generations of sailors have lived here since the dawning of the world. Centuries ago, Welsh vessels brought back copper and pilgrims from Ireland. Land and sea have always been closely linked and until recently the farmers were also fishermen, smugglers and sometimes pirates. Tenby is since two centuries the most important seaside resort of the mediterranean coast of Pembrokeshire. Its name comes from a variety of specific shells to be found in this region and is very much admired for its early bloom and the intensity of its colors.

At Strumble Head on the point closest to Ireland, a lighthouse was built. This small island can be reached by a bridge which links it to the continent.

*The sea on the coast of
Pembrokeshire, below and opposite
page bottom; and its countryside,
opposite page top right.
Strumble Head, opposite page top
left, is the closest point to Ireland.*

SNOWDONIA NATIONAL PARK

Snowdonia National Park comprises 350 km^2, bordered in the south by the sea and in the east by Gwyneld county. It is a mountainous region at an altitude of 1.085 meters. Walking, skiing, orientation courses, pony rides, fishing, canoeing, sailing are the principal attractions of the park. Furthermore, there are more than 1.500 paths to the mountain tops.

Betws y Coed is a charming mountain town which can be reached by train. The town has pleasantly adapted to the surrounding landscape and the suspension bridge is a romantic means to cross the river.

Llanberis pass is one of the most splendid sites of Snowdonia Park. From this pass little routes lead to the top of Snowdon Mountain.

Castle Harlech is a excellent example of military architecture. Built at the end of the 13th century, it used to be only accessible from the west side. Conquered and reconquered numerous times by the English and Welsh in the 15th century, it once induced a well-known Lancaster commander to give this famous comment:" I have occupied a French castle until all the old women of Wales had heard about it. I will occupy a Welsh castle until all the old women in France have had news about it."

Llanberis, above, is one of the most majestic regions of Snowdonia. Opposite page: top, the suspension bridge at Betws-y-Coed; below, Harlech Castle.

PORTMEIRION

This town is the architectural dream of Sir Clough Williams Ellis, who built it as a "living protest of wood and stone against the atrocities committed in the name of holy progress." Originally inspired by the town of Portofino, Portmerion mixes Georgian houses with a Jacobean city hall, Victorian facades, etcetera. Ernest Hemingway and Jean-Paul Sartre knew this town well.

THE LLEYN PENINSULA

The Lleyn peninsula is 25 kilometres long and between 5 and 16 kilometres wide. It is the Cape Finistere of Wales with Caernafon castle as one of its jewels. In Welsh the name Caer-yn-Arfon means 'fortress near Môn', i.e. near the island of Anglesey which borders Menai straits. Built on Roman foundations, this fortress is the work of the Norman Hughes D'Avranches, who in the 11th century was forced to turn the region over to the Welsh lords. Reconquered by Edward I one century later, this castle is the symbol of British power after the defeat of Llewelyn the Last.

Penrhyn castle, situated east of Bangor, is a fine sample of Norman-British Renaissance. Inside fine woodwork as well as delicate masonry can be admired. The style is Victorian. A bed made of a single bloc of slate is a curiosity.

Previous pages: Portmeirion.

Opposite page and this page above left: Penrhyn Castle.
This page above right and top: Caernarvon Castle. In Welsh Caernarvon means 'stronghold close to Menai' – in other words, close to the Isle of Anglesey.

In Wales, rugby is a cult.

Above and opposite page:

Aficionados of the oval ball in action.

RUGBY

In Wales, rugby is king and the players are demi-gods. Before the match the Welsh national anthem Hen Wlad fy Nhadau (Land of out Fathers) rings out, followed by Sospan Fach (the Little Saucepan), the 'national anthem' of Llanelli, and Calon Lan.

In the presence of the oval ball, all Welshmen transform themselves into tenors and baritones and the spectacle of the thousands of supporters who have come to cheer on the Red Devils of Cardiff remains an unforgettable memory. Some players – Cliff Morgan, Onwllywn Brace, Billy Cleaver, Mervyn Davies – have entered into legend.

The cult of rugby has its temple in the heart of the capital. Arms Park is situated in Westgate Street, a few yards from the principal commercial artery of Cardiff. It is here, too, that the Museum of Rugby can be found.

JEDBURGH

Kilt and bagpipes are inseparable from Scotland and this young Scots girl is perpetuating a tradition that goes back to the Middle Ages. In that epoch the 'kilt' was confined to a long length of tarten made from un-treated wool whose natural grease made the cloth waterproof. Envelo-ping the body, this toga-like garment had the colours and individual weave which were the distinct marks of a particular clan. The word clan is de-rived from clann – child in Gaelic – and denotes an integrated group of men, women and children under the authority of a chieftain. Destroyed politically after the disaster of Cullo-den (1746), which saw the defeat of the Scots at the hands of the English, the clan still survives symbolically in the heart and soul of every Scot.

Mary Queen of Scots lived in the manor built of huge stones, and it was from the same house that Mary Stuart galloped off to rejoin Both-well. A few relics have been faith-fully preserved – embroideries, her sewing basket and one of her death masks.

The small town of Jedburgh has hou-ses painted in pink, yellow, lavander and chocolate. Its abbey mirrors the monastic history of the Border re-gion. Building began on Jedburgh Abbey in 1140 and was completed in 1215. It was consecrated by monks who had come from Beauvais and King Malcolm IV was crowned there.

Opposite page: The residence of Mary Stuart.
This page: top, a bagpipes player; above, the tiny painted houses of Jedburgh.

Following pages: Sir Walter Scott's castle at Abbotsford.

ABBOTSFORD (THE HOUSE OF SIR WALTER SCOTT)

Together with Robert Burns, Walter Scott (1771-1832) is the most celebrated of Scottish writers. The youngest of a family of three, he spent his youth on his grandparents' farm near Melrose in the Border region. His fragile health confined him to the company of the womenfolk who enchanted him with popular culture and tales of brigands.

After successfully completing his studies at the University of Edinburgh, he opened a law practice but continued to champion the nostalgia of the Borders and their turbulent history. Waverley, his first novel, was directly inspired by a review of the family saga, improved somewhat by the imagination of an author who confirmed himself as one of the foremost romantics.

The success of this work led to the launch of an historical cycle (Ivanhoe, Quentin Durward) which assured him of glory. Walter Scott then gave up his career in Edinburgh and in 1812 retired to a modest farm, Cartleyhole, which – thanks to his author's royalties – he completely transformed.

Renamed Abbotsford, the house was furnished with the entrance hall of the palace of Linlithgow, panelling from Dumfermline and the ceiling of the chapel of Roslin. In the garden, Scott reproduced the cloister of Melrose Abbey. Because of his literary fame, Walter Scott was knighted by King George IV, but the bankrupty of his editor during a stock exchange crisis in 1826 left him in a precarious situation. He redoubled his efforts, driving himself hard until he was publishing three books a year. Worn out by overwork, he died on September 21st, 1832.

*Above: Melrose Abbey, founded by
monks of the Cluny order and
destroyed by Henry VIIIth.
Opposite page: top, the river Tweed,
where Sir Walter Scott loved to fish;
below, the fertile Melrose valley.*

MELROSE

The celebrated tweed cloth comes from this valley where the river Tweed has its source in the Southern Uplands. Walter Scott fished here and consumed his catch at the coaching inn at Clovenfords.

The quality of the wool of these herds gave rise to a textile industry which monks brought from Flanders and Picardy in the XIIth and XIIIth centuries. The first spinning mill dates back to 1750. At that time, a taste for mutton gave a considerable boost to sheep farming and to the wool industry.

Melrose Abbey is a haven of peace and religious serenity. It was founded by monks from Picardy who belonged to the order of Cluny. The fertility of the valley allowed the cultivation of barley and oats. The grass of the meadows provides essential nourishment for the sheep and, in turn, gives them their meat and wool. The Tweed is rich in fish and great markets, similar to those in Flanders, are held annually in the area.

But the message of peace and prosperity could not resist the assaults of Henry XIII who, furious at having been refused the hand of Mary Stuart in 1543, destroyed the abbey and ravaged the valley.

TRAQUAIR

Twenty-seven Scottish sovereigns have stayed at Traquair, the character of which transcends all the myths. 'No coaches, no cars, no dogs', warns a notice at the entrance. Tour operators are not welcome here. One comes to Traquair alone in order to perpetuate the memory of the Stuarts. Mary Stuart stayed here with Darnley in 1566. The master of Traquair was also the captain of her guard and since her visit a sombre, roughly-carved oaken door has borne the Scottish coat of arms. A genealogical tree commemorates the origin of the illustrious dynasty of Alexander of Macedonia. The reality of Traquair is symbolic, but the symbolism is very powerful. No concession has been made to modernity. The decor is rough, the walls whitewashed, the solid doors and staircases are as they were in the days of their glory. Electricity was not installed until 1962. The ground floor is damp and cold. Upstairs, the ceilings of the master apartments bear traces of a 16th-century painting. The harpsichord is once again in good repair.

In 1745, the last pretender to the throne, Bonnie Prince Charlie, took refuge here before the tragedy of Culloden and, according to Walter Scott, after the prince made his farewell the master of the house closed the gates and swore an oath not to open them again until the Stuarts regained the Scottish throne.

Above: The river Tweed flows past Traquair, where no cars or other vehicles are allowed. No concessions to modernity!
Opposite page: The house where Mary Stuart resided.

EDINBURGH, HOLYROOD PALACE

Originally Holyrood Palace was an abbey built by David 1 in 1128 to thank Providence for having saved his life by transforming the horns of a charging deer into a crucifix – Holy and Rood (cross in medieval English). The name has also been ascribed to the fragment of Christ's Cross given by Saint Margaret to her son, David. One of the many privileges enjoyed by the abbey, the right of sanctuary, was only lost in 1880. Until then, debtors hunted by the bailiffs regularly passed through its portals. Mary Stuart tried in vain to restore the refined ambiance she had known at the Court of Valois. It was here that her husband Darnley assassinated David Rizzio who had courted her a little too assiduously. When the Comte D'Artois (the future Charles X of France) emigrated during the Revolution, it was Holyrood in which he found shelter.

In 1822, George IV, the first British king of the House of Hanover, came to Scotland, installed himself at Holyrood and appeared in a kilt at a court ball. Queen Victoria visited Holyrood and Queen Elizabeth II stays here whenever she visits Edinburgh.

Holyrood, built in the Middle Ages, is the oldest palace in Europe to have been continuously inhabited by monarchs.

Above: Castle Rock which dominates Edinburgh.
Top and opposite page middle: Holyrood Palace, the oldest royal residence in Europe.
Opposite page: top and bottom, two details of the unicorn on the facade of Holyrood Palace.

EDINBURGH

The capital of Scotland, Edinburgh can be particularly appreciated at nightfall when the walls and towers of the castle on top of its great basalt pedestal are illuminated. Rock Castle is built on an extinct volcano. The first people to fortify the place were the soldiers of Edwin, King of Norway, who gave his name to the site – Edwin's burgh (hill).

Bloody battles between the kings of England and Scotland took place here because the castle, guarded by three cliff faces and seven lines of defence, was so impregnable.

Edinburgh Castle has been the stage of sparkling pageant and bloody drama such as the execution, during the course of a banquet, of two pretenders to the throne of the young king, James Stuart II, then only ten years old.

Napoleon's officers were imprisoned in the castle and Mary Stuart gave birth here. Each summer, on the esplanade, the spectacular Military Tattoo takes place.

1600 metres separate Castle Rock from Holyrood Palace. High Street marks the Royal Mile of old Edinburgh.

The new city was built after 1760 around these old monuments, seperated from them by broad avenues. The prosperity of the 19th century resulted in great development in Edinburgh, but the city remained faithful to the Neo-Classical style which earned it the name of 'the New Athens'. The arts museums and the celebrated festival make the city particularly attractive.

Top: Edinburgh at night, the castle illuminated.
Above: Two of the city's monuments.
Opposite page: The Mining Museum.

GLASGOW

Based on the number of inhabitants, Glasgow is the third largest city in Great Britain and the largest in Scotland. It spreads along the length of the Clyde, crossed by road and rail bridges, and is surrounded by lochs.

In the beginning there was Saint Mungo. Arriving from Ireland, the hermit built a wooden church in 534, and this became a cathedral in the grand Gothic style of the 13th century. David 1 installed a bishop's palace in 1115 and the university was established in 1540. In the Middle Ages the city was an important centre of commerce, trading with England and Europe. In the 18th century, the exploitation of coal allowed the city to become a centre of heavy industry and shipbuilding. The shipyards were among the most important in the world and the Queen Mary and Queen Elizabeth were built here.

Glasgow is a commercial city which has always adapted to the needs of its

economic development. John Knox introduced Protestantism, but was not successful in burning down the cathedral, as he was in the habit of doing. The people opposed his decision and the cathedral was saved. When the Act of Union was signed in 1707, patriotic Scots were forced to accept that the merchants of Glasgow had dealings with the English and they departed for the colonies in America and Asia where they sought their fortune. Sailing ships left Glasgow for the New World, loaded with manufactured products, and returned with cargoes of sugar, rum and especially tobacco, over which the city exercised a quasi-monopoly.

George Square, in the centre of town, is situated at the foot of the hill where the school buildings and the University of Strasthelyde are located.

The Clyde, flowing through Glasgow, is spanned by many bridges.
Top: The Forth Road bridge
Above: The Railway bridge.
Opposite page: middle, Saint Mungo's Cathedral in Glasgow; bottom, Georges Square.

Above: Stirling and the Forth valley.
Opposite page: The statue of
William Wallace, hero of Scottish
independence, erected at the corner
of the keep of the Wallace Monument,
the tower of which is 75 metres tall.

STIRLING

Over the centuries many roads have led to Stirling, strategic city which controls the gateway between the Lowlands and the Highlands. "He who holds Stirling Castle, holds the Scottish nation," it was said. In 1297, William Wallace defied the English and in 1314 Robert Bruce repulsed the armies of Edward II at Bannockburn, four kilometres south of the town.

After regaining independence the Stuarts made Stirling Castle their residence. James IV, man of the Renaissance, furnished the royal apartments there. On the ceiling of the Queen's Chamber are forty sculptured wooden medaillons representing kings, queens and personages from the Bible as well as Greek mythology.

Today, Stirling Castle still keeps guard over the old city and the valley of the Forth. Three kilometres away, on the summit of a small hill, the Wallace Monument has been raised. The tower is seventy-five metres in height. It was erected in 1869 and is dedicated to the memory of William Wallace, hero of the struggle for Scottish independence. His statue, nestling in an angle of the walls of the donjon, holds a burning sword. It was at Stirling, in the church of the Holy Rude, where Mary Stuart was crowned in 1543 and where her son, James, was baptised.

PERTH

Celebrated for its 'Fair Maid' which inspired a novel by Sir Walter Scott and an opera by Georges Bizet, Perth is a ravishing provincial city situated in a verdant pastoral valley on the Firth of Tay.

Perth was the first capital of the Kingdom of Scotland after Kenneth Mac Alpine united the Picts and Scots in 896. Having brought from the Holy Land a stone which, according to legend, had served as Jacob's pillow, Kenneth installed it as the symbol of Scots royalty. It was on the stone of Scone, set at the gates of Perth, that most of the Scottish kings were crowned. In 1297, Edward I carried it to Westminster from where, in 1950, students of Glasgow University managed to remove it and return it to Scotland, where it remained for several months.

In Curfew Road, the Fair Maid's House has several ancient objects and examples of traditional Scottish craftsmanship. Balhousie Castle, built in the 15th century, and considerably rebuilt in the last century, houses the Black Watch Regimental Museum. The Black Watch, an elite regiment, was created in 1725 by General Wade to contain the Highlanders.

Above: The towers and belltowers of Perth, a town which possesses the Stone of Scone, brought back from the Holy Land and dating from the year 846.
Opposite page: Balhousie Castle houses the Black Watch Regimental Museum.

LOCH NESS

Though the existence of Nessie has been denied by many, the saga of the celebrated monster continues to haunt the banks of Loch Ness. Its first appearance dates back to 565 when Saint Adaman reported the presence of a strange animal. In 1934, a retired colonel announced that he had made 42 sightings between 1923 and 1933. In 1957, another book, by Constance White, made reference to 60 sightings. A large number of works can be consulted at the Loch Ness Monster Exhibition Centre on the shores of the lake. Fort Augustus Abbey was founded in 1876. Built for the Benedictines, it is integrated into Fort Augustus, a military fortification dedicated to William Augustus, Duke of Cumberland, third son of George II of England and victor at Culloden over Bonnie Prince Charlie (1746).

LOCH LOMOND

Situated 30 kilometres from Glasgow Loch Lomond is the largest of the Scottish lochs (35 kilometres long and 8 kilometres wide at its broadest point). It once sheltered hermits along its banks and on its islands. Today, it is a resort for the people of Glasgow who go there to fish and to practise various watersports.

Fort August Abbey, above, on the shores of Loch Ness, does not declare war on the monster that lurks in its waters. The waters, opposite page, which mirror the sky and which offer excellent sailing and fishing.

Following pages: Loch Lomond, the biggest of the Scottish lochs.

GLENCOE

This beautiful site is protected by the National Trust of Scotland, but its granduer cannot erase the memory of one of the bloodiest episodes in the history of Scotland, the massacre of the Macdonalds by the Campbells.

After failing in their bid to restore the Stuarts to the throne, the rebel Jacobites obtained the pardon of King George III, a Hanovarian. But in exchange he demanded that the Highland clans swore an oath of allegiance and fidelity before January 1st, 1692. The Macdonalds, who had established their quarters in the valley of Glencoe, swore their oath on January 6th. Taking this tardiness as an affront, the king decided to make an example of them and dispatched Campbell of Glenlyon to take revenge.

After having been generously received by the Macdonalds, the Campbells massacred 38 of them at dawn on January 13th by setting fire

to the houses in which they had received such friendly hospitality.

Every year, on January 13th, a commemorative mass is held at the foot of a Celtic cross erected 'in memory of McIan, chief of the MacDonalds of Glencoe, who fell with his people in the massacre of Glencoe.'

In the village of Glencoe, on the banks of Loch Leven, there is a museum where various Jacobite relics are on display.

Above: The ochre cliffs which rise above Loch Lomond.
Top: Loch Leven.
Opposite page: the mountains around Glencoe, a region protected by the National Trust of Scotland.

ABERDEEN

Situated above latitude 57° north, Aberdeen is not only the 'Granite City', but also the 'Silver City' and 'the Flower of Scotland'. The stones of its houses were cut from the local quarries and they have also been used in the construction of churches, bridges and, it is said, half the tombs in Scotland.

Once, the cod and the herring provided the riches of a port which traded actively with the ports of the Baltic. Today Aberdeen is particularly known as 'the oil capital' thanks to the North Sea oil fields situated near the Orkneys.

In 1975, Queen Elizabeth inaugurated the pipeline which carried the production of the first platforms to the coast and by 1977 the North Sea oil fields (244,000 km2) provided 40% of Great Britain's consumption. In 1982, offshore drilling assured 50% of British Petroleum's requirements and, in 1988, 10% of world production. The activity of the port consists of 40% oil, 10% fishing and the rest in maritime transport.

An austere and industrious city whose inhabitants have the reputation of being thrifty, Aberdeen offers charming flower gardens and parks.

Above: Aberdeen park and (top) the Aberdeen harbour.
Opposite page: Aberdeen Town Hall. All the houses in the city are built of granite. These have given Aberdeen the name of the 'silver city'.

THE GRAMPIAN HIGHLANDS

The Grampian Highlands, in the north-east of Scotland, have a strong personality and agricultural land celebrated for its prime beef. The Scottish cow, furnished with a formidable pair of horns, long-haired and savage, seems an almost prehistoric animal.

In the far north the Highlands offer a mountainous landscape, usually deserted. It is the domain of a hard life, the badger and the eagle. People come here to shoot grouse.

The Grampian Highlands are evidence of Scotland's formidable Scottish geological history. One could easily compare the succession of reliefs to a succession of strophes derived from the creation of the elements which particularly inspired the poet Norman Mac Caig.

This region of Scotland has countryside which is among the most powerful and most secretive in Europe. The luxuriant river valleys, especially that of the Spey, at the foot of the mountains and amid woodlands and pastures, serve as a natural backcloth for the distillation of Scotch malt whisky.

The Northern Highlands, above, have a wild and secret nature, which inspired the poet Norman MacCaig. Opposite page: a typical farm of the region.

INVERNESS

Inverness is situated at the mouth of the river Ness and its name literally means 'mouth of the Ness'. It is the gateway between the Northern Highlands and the rest of Scotland. Historically, Saint Columba converted king Pict Brude here in 565. Macbeth built a fortress here in 1507 which was destroyed by Malcolm Canmore after he had vanquished him.

In Victorian times this fortress, nothing of which remains, became the foundation for the construction of this edifice which dominates the town. In its gardens is a statue of Flora Macdonald, counsellor to the Jacobites during their attempt to restore the Stuarts, in the person of Bonnie Prince Charlie, to the throne. It commemorates an heroic but bloody page in Scottish history, a page which ended at Cuulloden on April 16th, 1746. The Highlanders of Charles Edward Stuart were crushed by the troops of the Duke of Cumberland. The battle only lasted 40 minutes and 1500 of the dead are buried on the battlefield. The massacre gave the Duke of Cumberland his name of 'Butcher of Culloden'.

The Scottish prince managed to escape with a few of his officers and a little later embarked for the Isle of Skye where Flora Macdonald facilitated his flight. The statue of Flora the Courageous is in Inverness. On the west bank of the Ness stands the cathedral of Saint Andrew.

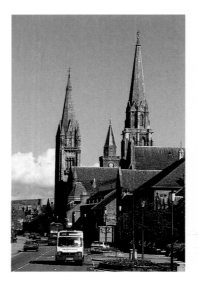

Opposite page: Saint Andrew's Cathedral in Inverness.
This page: top, the statue of Flora Macdonald; above left, Bank Street; and right, in remembrance of the

Battle of Culloden where Prince Charles Edward and his troops were utterly defeated by the Duke of Cumberland, surnamed the 'Butcher of Culloden'.

THE ISLE OF SKYE

The Hebrides are a collection of islands situated off the west coast of Scotland. To get to Skye, the largest island, one embarks at Lochalsh. The trip takes no more than five minutes. To experience the emotions of the journey, some people prefer to take the boat from Mallaig for Armadale. Known as the isle of heather, Skye covers an area of 155 km^2 and its highest point is 1000 metres above sea level. The history of the island, peopled by rough warriors and audacious sailors, is that of the clans who clashed over the centuries, before the mass emigration to Glasgow or Nova Scotia.

Rough warriors who never forgot that 'Liberty and whisky are the same' as Robert Burns remarked. Invented in Ireland, it is said that the recipe for whisky was brought to Scotland by monks. Five hundred years ago, the Gaelic reference 'wisge beatha' (water of life) first appeared in the texts. Whisky is the result of distillation, but in particular of a mysterious alchemy between the air, the water flowing from the glens, the barley and the peat. Harvested in August, the barley is first laid out on planks to germinate. The malt is then dried in an oven fired by peat before being ground and mixed with water to make an infusion which allows the dissolving and retention of sugar. The liquid obtained is then poured into barrels and mixed with yeast which provokes an intense fermentation which lasts 48 hours. The product is then heated and distilled in a copper still until it attains an alcohol percentage of between 43% and 57% per litre. A good whisky must be aged for at least 8 years in wooden barrels which previously contained sherry or port.

Opposite page middle: Embarking at Lochalsh for the Isle of Skye. Above and opposite page top: A whisky distillery. It is said that the excise duties were paid by monks in Scotland for five centuries.

CONTENTS

INDEX

PHOTO CREDITS